Testimonials from Online friends (clients)

<u>Candy Elena Araujo</u> with <u>Lavender Lily</u> (my facebook name)

Thank u for being a godsend to me. your reading was very much on point and well worth the donation.

Leah

Daisy is my favorite reader on Oranum. She connects with me and my situation and gives wonderful advice

.

mistie1

She is great and always open hearted I always have great readings from her she speaks the truth and guides you of what can help you and give you strength. San diego cal.

JBee

She's really good. Picked up on my situation very well and gave me clarity. 5 stars all the way.

New york | 2013-10-12 07:18:23

Mark

One of the best readers on oranum. 5 stars is a understatement. Mark is now one of my Online Best-ies I do readings for him monthly

Just a teeny tiny glimpse of my online friends

Table of contents:

WHAT YOU WILL RECEIVE FROM MY "WORK FROM HOME AS A SUCCESSFUL PSYCHIC" GUIDE.

You will acquire thorough "researched" hands on Experience and Knowledge through many years of strategy, testing, spiritual growth, mind-full expansion, and infinite "ACTION".

DEFINISITION = you get to eat the gourmet delicacy without having to lose precious time and energy over a hot oven. Enjoy the delightful-ness while I do all the work for you.

Through the pages of my "work from home guide" I will illustrate how my passionate a hobby streams an income of over $5,000 a month.

"YOU CAN & WILL ACHIEVE IT TOO".

Joys of a successful psychic:

Living an Abundant life, while working on "YOUR" schedule.

Make money while you sleep or take the day OFF and still earn.

*****The most popular question****

How do I get Clients?

My researched (proven) strategies are simple and abundantly "STRONG" this is YOUR year for "SUCCESS" as a psychic.

I Daisy Fabelo welcome you to a Multi-Million dollar Growing industry that touches the lives of millions year round.

"EVERYONE IS LOOKING FOR GUIDANCE" Looking for "YOU".

****Most popular question Number 2****

"What's your SECRET?

My secret is so simple you'll ask Wow why didn't I think of that or "HA' I knew that= SUCCESS all inside this quirky little How to Guide.

Successful psychic Videos:

http://www.youtube.com/playlist?list=PLfS4AILZV-vlyOuN1IL_4movrNxnhamZK

I am ignited to share with you my successful psychic videos for FREE as I promised.

The reason behind my grateful-ness is due to all the years of waiting for success. Researching for the best source of income and it truly wasn't until 2011 that I truly am highly successful. I mean making $1,000- $2,000 is great source of income but making over $5,000 dollars a month now that is something to be proud of. Yet it is not all the quality time I share with my family that is what I call a "RICH PSYCHIC" you can have millions in the bank but if you don't have LOVE then $$$money doesn't really matter.

I advice that you subscribe yourself to my YouTube channel videos, as new ones are being created this lovely month of May 2014 and all the time. Our world has shifted in its entirety I am honored to be part of this massive wave of abundant success. The angels have asked me to share all my knowledge with you. The main point of being a successful psychic is due to research.

You need to be constantly researching your career. As my career is all about being a spiritual teacher, advisor (psychic), I research this genre all the time.

I ask my angels and spiritual guides for the knowledge that I need in order to serve humankind my brothers and humanly sisters.

This is what you will find in my book TRUTH, because I am always eager to learn and then excited to share.

In my line of videos you will learn how I capture my online friends (audience) through personal touch. If and when you want to start your very own video streams you need to be personal and yourself. It is important to be truthful.

Working as an online psychic is a highly successful way to make a living from the comfort of your home. As it is a rewarding way to spread beautiful messages that heal and guide others onto beautiful paths.

Within this very book you will learn how to be an online psychic, among the endless paths of a spiritual light worker; the best tools needed for the trade, where to apply for a free and start working this same week.

I have worked as an online psychic since 2007 today I make $1000.oo every two weeks and that's just from my online psychic job. Not counting the readings I do through Skype, face book, YouTube, phone, email and as a party entertainer.
I will teach you everything you need, where to buy the tools for the best prices, how to grow spiritually, and what are the highest paid psychic secrets.

"HOW IT ALL STARTED" Believing the Impossible is possible. Key#1

When I first discovered working from home in 1996 I never knew that I could make double what my stressful nine-five was bringing.

I researched and fell many times, up until 2007. When I found my inner voice and decided to do only what I love and love what I do.

I have been reading friends for years and as I grew spiritually my knowledge, intuition and confidence grew too. In the beginning I felt that this was a gift and I should not charge. Then as I kept transforming I learned that like any trade there needs to be an exchange. When we work we get paid getting paid is not negative. With money we buy the things we want and need. The same falls under working as a psychic. My son says mom you are a spiritual advisor and in many ways I am. People come to me for advice; to know what might be coming in their lives. It is like an insight to what could be and what you need to be aware of; in order to create the best possible outcome. Imagine if you knew each week what was coming emotionally, physically, mentally. What would you do with this knowledge?

"Everyone seeks guidance". You are the guide.

Key #2

My clients look for my weekly YouTube channel readings where I give insights into the next week of their lives of our lives. My YouTube subscribers are growing weekly I started with less than ten and I am at over 222 subscribers.

https://www.youtube.com/user/daisyf1305

In other words one of the best secrets a psychic holds is a YouTube channel. Within YouTube you start a fan base or what I call online friends. They become familiar with you, see you as your neighbor, your aunt, your old friend. I find that being personal with my online friends makes us comfortable and as I am truly a loving person this comes truly easy for me.

Put yourself in your online friend's shoes. Would you seek a psychic that is loving, friendly or would you go to someone cold and dull?

YouTube is a great place to build your business by not only promoting yourself but showing your talent. Today people are still holding tight to their money. You need to show your gifts, your energy, to truly capture the hearts of your online friends that will "SHARE" you. This is the best kept secret "SHARING" when your videos are viewed and liked and shared YouTube ranks you higher and your videos are now seen by more and more each week.

Now work your magik over your videos. You need to share everything on your about section in each video. Yes this is a bit time consuming. What you could do is write out a word copy of all your info, prices, face book pages, blogs, email, etsy, WebPages. Everything you sell and how your readings are provided.

I am also creating a line of videos on "How to live the psychic life" on my YouTube channel. In this category I provide a detailed how to guide where I show my stuff. I share from the spells to the readings and everything In between. I also share psychics off so you are more than welcome to come over and share your gifts with all your ratings. This is why I share YouTube first because it's my #1.

BLOGTALK RADIO:
I have come across a few of you that are not comfortable in front of the Video. There is a great place for your talents and it is free to start. http://www.blogtalkradio.com/daisyf1305

In blogtalk radio you can have as many live radio shows for half hour time frames. All you need is your computer and your phone. Online friends will call in to talk to you the show host. Be creative with your shows and share all your info because you want to be available for paid readings. Believe me after a few Live Shows your online friends want MORE!!! They will seek you for readings within your work time. I have been so busy these past few months because I use YouTube and Blogtalk radio. You can too!!!

Expanding from just an online psychic to creating your very own tools: Key #3

Now I know you want to get right to it. You want the link to the job. I want you to be prepared. I want you to see in the many ways I have expanded my path and how you can too. Deep within we are all artist, reading online is a form of art you are listening to your heart regardless if it's through simple cards that give thorough messages. Using pendulums, ruins, crystals, or any form of spiritual tools.

I have created my very own oracle cards to make my readings very personal. I know exactly what each card means, because I have painted them, I have added personal messages to them.

I also sell them to my clients, and online friends (I do not like to call people followers or fans because if they believe what I inspire then they are friends, therefore online friends or earth angels are everyone I work with online). My oracle cards sell for $25.00 through etsy, eBay, and YouTube. As I am updating my eBook my cards are being published by a successful company in Australia. The reason I share my success is so that you can become inspired and see the many wings you can grow successfully as an online psychic. I started painting my cards in early 2011 and my angels advised that they be completed before 2012. Though they were challenging I feel now that my angels were pushing me to complete a major task. I had deadlines and all by November 2011 my first set was complete.

 Yet the work is never quite complete I am still adding to the cards, more in depth messages, more vibrant colors, better printers. This is a great way for those of you intuitive beings that also enjoy artful methods of creativity.

You can start creating your very own oracle cards that you can use with your online friends.

Imagine now not only do you work as an online psychic but now you have cards that you have created and you are able to sell; bringing in even more income, expanding your online friends through sales of your art work, while sharing beautiful messages.

Word of mouth (key #4)

Word of mouth is the very best way to create a lucrative business for you. This is all done from everything described above and by your beautiful online friends. See your testimonials will create a POSITIVE REVIEW and your online friends will be your PROOF. In the beginning of this little Guide I showed off some of my favorite testimonials. One because they truly make me "HAPPY" and Inspire both you and my new online friends, =potential clients. See they loved the reading you gave on YouTube but it wasn't enough so they'll say, "This is a great online friend". Who will be able to give me the guidance I seek or need. Then they'll run over to their friends and say. "You know my psychic friend helped me out of a situation and you will help you too. Wa la new online friends. The secret is YOU being YOU. I am honest I am me with all my flaws and grammar issues but I know That my True online friends will look over look the misspells and read my work and share my research because we have connected we have rapport together and this my friend is the secret.

Then there's FIVERR, a great way to get everything done. Today you are a successful online psychic, your tools are growing and you don't have time to do everything. Fiverr is your answer. ***Fiverr: the way to outsource and give to others that are working from home.***

http://fiverr.com

When I need my eBooks to get views Fiverr, when I need editing done fiverr, let's say you want to create your own oracle cards you know exactly how you want them done, but you're not the best artist, fiverr. The positive thing about outsourcing is giving, by paying others for their work. I love Fiverr because the best part is the gigs start at $5.00 now that's a deal. And you are doing something positive you are helping others work from home. You are now not just a work from home successful psychic but an employer. Many eBook writers get their work edited through Fiverr. Online friends are a great way to outsource the completed job you seek. Face book friends always know someone that edits or artist eager to paint your cards.

The best tools, the ones I use personally and positively. (Key #6)

When I first started reading to friends I used angel messages, I love angels after all they are the messengers of GOD. Angels give positive, loving, inspirational advice. Now they do explain the cons but in loving manners. I do not like the dark arts; I do not work with anything negative, no black magic, nothing evil. All love all angels, mystical creatures, fairies, elementals, all love; all for the greater good. The best part about working under love is that your online friends will come to you just because of that. You will want to study the best in the trade like Doreen Virtue. Doreen has a PHD in angel messages. She not only lives from her spirituality she creates her own card decks and I love to use them. As you grow and become comfortable and confident you can look for your own tools. Always follow your intuition when choosing your tools. http://www.amazon.com/Daily-Guidance-Angels-Oracle-Cards/dp/1401907725/ref=sr_sp-

The daily Guidance oracle cards give a clear message, you don't have to fidget with the book to get the message it's all right in front of you.

Now everyone needs this set of cards, these cards are the ones that will bring you the money. They flow and the pictures are vivid remember when reading oracle cards it's really important to follow your intuition. The colors pictures are other forms of messages look in depth and see what the angels are saying.

Doreen Virtues Romance deck is a must. The romance deck is going to be your money maker. These cards dabble within the love life and most of the people that come to you wanting readings need a clear image about their love life. Does he love me, will she marry me, when will I meet him, how will she be? What's going on in my marriage am I being lied to? These are among the many questions I receive. The best part about becoming an online psychic through me is I have a video course that will show you exactly how it's done and if you need further instruction you can receive personal videos for your specific questions. Now that's what I call thorough.

Add me on face book "MYSTIC ANGEL READINGS AND SPIRITUAL ADVICE" you can personally message me there.

https://www.facebook.com/pages/Mystic-Angel-readings-and-spiritual-advice/212860072104259

Another great deck of cards that have helped me clarify many of my online friends is the angel tarot. The angel tarot has guided work, finance, spirituality, love, health; it is an extremely positive deck. Though what I love about the deck is that if something is not right this deck will let you know. I truly advice my online friends with positive assurance with this deck and they are grateful. I recommend this amazing Tarot made by Doreen and Valentine the original Tarot creator of today. Please try to purchase your tools new. If you do not, I advice a simple cleansing and re-charging technique, first place your tools in the moonlight. I put my cards next to my altar over the windowsill. I leave them for one night and one day to cleanse and re-charge when cards are over loaded. For new cards I advice to do this for seven days and six nights. You can even add sage over the cards for a more powerful cleansing. When I do smudging within my home especially around my work place I smudge right over all my tools.

More tools:

Since you are starting you need a few crystals to open up those psychic channels.

I recommend amethyst, which brings clarity and you want to be clear in order to read your online friends. Also amethyst is used as protection, healing, it attracts positive energy.

You can purchase your amethyst through Amazon, eBay, even face book. I have done many purchases through eBay but truly enjoy buying through psychic fairs, and mystical stores. When you walk up to the stones, and or crystals that call your attention you will notice some calls are stronger than others. It's like they become brighter or even stand out, that is the one you want to purchase.

I just purchased selenite because of the higher frequency to the spirit world and it is great for healing, transmute, and lucid dreams that I work with as visions to write messages that come through. Selenite is very special because they can cleanse and clear other stones and crystals. I purchased a wand and a sphere (you can see them in my YouTube videos) they are great with clarity, visions, healing, and my favorite to increase psychic ability.

Rainbow fluorite works great with manifesting good things into your life quickly. It is a great stone to work with in meditation, transmute negative energy into positive energy. That is a really important when working with people because some have really negative energies and you don't want to pick them up. Rainbow fluorite is great at protecting your energy. Keep it close I like to wear mine in a lovely necklace that one of my FAV online friends made for me. Both selenite and rainbow fluorite clear your third eye.

These are just a few of my favorite that I recommend as you continue on your spiritual path you will learn which tools fit your personally transforming needs.

As your endeavor grows you want to keep adding to your beautiful work place. I recommend that you research crystal for your personal self. We all have spiritual traits, elements, and our solar and birth signs. Finding crystals to work with can be as simple as going to a metaphysical shop and seeking through energy allowing the law of attraction to guide you to the perfect crystals. I am now studying the art of crystal readings and working with stones and crystals, next venture.

Creating an altar: To work as an online psychic you need a professional background you want your clients to seek you as a successful professional

psychic or how I like to call myself spiritual advisor. (key #7)

You need to find an area within your home that is quiet, clean, clutter free one where you can add a beautiful back ground. Use your creativity when you create your altar as I love to call it. My altar as seen above changes during different seasons I love to adorn with flowers angels, and decorations. I enjoy decorating my working altar this is what my online friends see when I am working. Be creative and thrifty within my eBook

http://www.amazon.com/Work-Spiritual-Path-Daisy-Fabelo-ebook/dp/B00DXH6ZUG

I have a whole chapter on where to find FREE office supplies, furniture, etc. As we are creating a spiritual altar the same applies. You need to be SAVVY. Go to flea markets, check neighbors trash, go to the rich neighborhoods, they love to discard awesome goodies. I once found a whole display of pet supplies for parakeets, the cage, food, toys, stand, all new.

As the back drop of my altar I was lucky because my brother let me borrow his beautiful curtain that is celestial sun moon, and stars. IDEA: go to Wal-mart, K-Mart, Target, Ross, TJMAxx, Marshalls, among other outlets find the home goods and look at the sales merchandise. You'll want the curtains, thin spreads, fabrics; use your creative eye to find a lovely background for your spiritual work area. I just added some fun lights with stars and those adorable Holiday lights.

Success story: Sage Goddess

https://www.facebook.com/SageGoddess

Sage Goddess is a true inspirational story just like you and me she had a dream. That started as she shares from an intention. Today she has 1000's of reviews her Etsy shop has exploded with prosperity and people from all over have her magical products.

Imagine you today start your very own line of spiritual products using inspiration from ideas adding your artful touch and Ka-Bam you are a successful psychic. She founded her face book page in 2010 today she has not only sold across the world through etsy but she has just opened her shop. You can be this beautiful success story too.

Quote from Sage Goddess "*What begins as a wish and dream can grow wings and fly. Sage Goddess began as a single intention set at a new moon just over 2 years ago. Thank you to the 40,000 of you who are now with me on this magical journey. I am grateful to each of you and wish you abundant joy, peace, and health. May you be blessed. May we bless each other. So it is.*"

*(key #8)*Today is your day what is your intention? What is your desire? You can do this too. The gifts I receive and add to my altar all come through intention. I put the intention that I would like to add something and the Universe takes care of the details.

My Angels are from everywhere the large one was my very first angel she was a gift, the smaller one was from Walgreens she was only $1.29. Do the walking you shall be guided to find exactly what you need at the price to fit your needs.

My table is covered so it looks lovely. Truth is the table is nothing more than one of those eating stands that you use when you're watching television. They are three for $20.00 at Wal-Mart. I just purchased a shelf at Target for less than $30.00 as I make money I add more tools, and my online friends love to see my goodies and use them.

Today my altar is in a beautiful condo on the beach where I can easily access the element of water. It is a dream come true made real by my success that now I share with you.

What is your dream? It too will come true."
LINK to your psychic online job: What you have
been waiting for. Key #9

I work for Oranum, if you go to my blog
http://theworkfromhomemuse.blogspot.com/
You will find numerous posts on Oranum and if you
want to start the application process even before
finishing reading this little book here's the link:

http://registration.oranum.com/master_account.ph p?partner=esmeralda1305 Now this is an easy process and I will walk you through your interview. First you will fill out an easy application add your experience BE DETAILED.

What you will need:

You need fast internet that plugs into your computer no wireless.

You need a webcam and microphone (I used my computer webcam and microphone but they are growing and want you to work professionally Today I use the Logitech webcam that you can purchase on eBay for a fraction of the price). Your spiritual back ground, a professional picture of you digitally uploaded.

As soon as you start you will be able to work on your profile they want a video where you sell yourself, what gifts you have, your specialties, etc. Pretty simple right as soon as all that is ready you will be able to start, they are eager for you to start working on Oranum. One of my latest mentees has made $500.00 in her first two weeks.

Imagine how much you can make. I have a calendar where I set my goals for how much I want to make within the time frame.

#1 how do you get paid:

I guess I should have explained this one first right? Payment is up to you Oranum pays through many different venues you can receive a check that you will arrive approx the 15th and the 30th of each month.

You can use the credit card payoneer (this is what I use because you get paid FAST) issue with payoneer they charge for everything. If you take out money, to make the money available straight away, monthly fees; but since they are so fast I don't mind the fees. There is wire transfer but the fee is ridiculous. You can find all of this through the knowledge base Q&A section of your personal Oranum. *The interview:*

This will be the easiest interview because it's all through Skype. You use your tools and give a reading of choice and BANG your set to start right after your interview, as long as you have all your tools. THE main thing they check is the fast access internet because they don't want you to lag during readings.

After you work for the period they tell you there will be a second interview just like the first. PLUS a TEST!!!!!! Scary right NO!!!!! The test is based on the knowledge Q & A you can take your time and find the answers.

This is what I did:

I read through everything because you want to know all the rules, first so clients don't take advantage of you and second so you can keep your job. Then while on the test I went back and forth and made sure the answers were correct since I had already read everything I knew exactly where to look. After Oranum moderators approve you, then you can set your per minute rate. Now there are Oranum workers that charge $9.99 a min. I charge in this manner. In the beginning of the week I charge $1.99 a minute after the 2oth I charge $1.49 the min. The reason for this is because, I am searched more from newbie's for quick and cheap readings, therefore when I am on I am always making money.

Of course once you start working you can feel around and charge what you like I don't work too many hours therefore I am less expensive to make sure everyone that seeks my spiritual advice is able to afford me.

FREE CHAT/PRIVATE CHAT:

Okay FREE CHAT is where you are engaged with everyone I have had over fifty people in my room at one time everyone wants your attention and sometimes it can be overwhelming.

What to do?

Engage in a conversation a topic that will grab your members, I give message cards that give inspirational messages. Normally when I do this someone will take me too private straight away.

YOU DO NOT GIVE FREE READINGS IN FREE CHAT: First because you are not getting paid, second because they will drive you nuts and lastly ORANUM no, no....

This is what I tell them, I can't give free readings because there is no energy exchange, plus since there are too many in the room the energies can mix and you won't receive an accurate reading and my credibility is on the line. YOU CAN DO MEDITATIONS for them, play music, pray, and give one card message.

Feel around for your personal way to work.

One of the things I did when I first started was go to other Oranum virtual rooms and see how they worked. I even get readings with other members its fun and a learning experience. PRIVATE: private is how you get paid you want your client to be in private for as long as possible you want them wanting more. HERE"S MY ISSUES: I am quick and I don't steal if I am done, if there is nothing else I don't hold up my Oranum Clients. I have many regulars that just want someone to hear them. They get a reading and then they vent, this is why I call myself a spiritual advisor, they want my personal advice therefore my advice is always positive, loving, guided, from GOD>>>>

I usually give a thorough reading in ten min. but I have regulars that have stayed with me for 80 min. As you get comfortable you can work your magic. Honesty works for me I don't give specific answers like for ex: Will I get pregnant? Am I pregnant? I give them a reading about their questions the angels are great at giving specific messages but no right spot on answers I am not a medium I talk with angels.

Do you see me married? Will he leave me? AGAIN I give them an overview; I let them ask questions and answers as best as the angels answer.

YOU WILL HAVE SOME WHO WILL NOT BE HAPPY>

I had one client who got a reading from me and was upset because in the reading the guy that she was with had left her and it showed he wasn't coming back. She was upset because another member told her she was to marry the guy. MY ANSWER: we have free will, if she leaves me at that moment runs to the guy takes him with all his flaws and he accepts her they can get married. I say what the angels message, you want honesty not a pretty picture because if I sugar coat everything then my clients won't come for my honesty. I am love but you are here for clarity. She came back a few months later and said he didn't come back and she had moved on to a new love. DON"T FEEL BAD they will make you sometimes feel guilty and question yourself because they want to hear something specific and what they want to hear. *KEEP the flow in your room:*

Remember you are the face of Oranum, engage with all your personality I love to guide, I talk about the latest books I am reading, shows I am watching movies etc. I am personal with my oranum clients I make them feel like I am Esmeralda a friend they can come and hang out with. I drink tea, and coffee

with them. I read passages from my books; I share on attracting good-ness in their lives. I HAVE HELPED 1000's and that's my BLISS!!!!!!
NOW don't stop at Oranum there are multitudes of psychic jobs. Truth is I barely work at oranum because I am in a place where everyone simply finds me. Therefore I simply let everyone know when I am available and they fill up my reading appointments.

CREATE A FACEBOOK PAGE: (key #10)My face book pages where word of mouth has send me many online friends where they message me every few months for updates on their life. I give them the power to donate whatever they want. The least amount I have received has been $11.00. I have charged $5.00 to someone that was really broke and of course I help many who are in need, for that's my BLISS.

The universal gifts are infinite I have received stones, necklaces, tools, planners, books, and many other gifts. They always take care of me; I have been sent shells, a lovely fluorite necklace that I use all the time. I have been sent gift cards, many online friends, and new members for ORANUM... I know other spiritual psychics who make jewelry where each piece is for something specific, they have oils, waters, candles and so on. The thing is be creative, I know one woman who has her spiritual store right from her home, where she does readings and sells her merchandise and other friends merchandise. She is very successful.

Subscribe on my blog as you will be emailed when I write new posts and I share what other moms are doing from home, in this manner you get ideas and perfect your own. Once again here the link great luck and positive endeavors send me your email so I can send you the videos on How to be a successful psychic:

http://registration.oranum.com/master_account.php?partner=esmeralda1305

Living the psychic life's dream. This little eBook has been a dream to me. I have connected with thousands and feel my words within these pages grow like a flower blooms through the Florida lands. I started to write this book to share how awesome and easy it is to work from your passion. If you are still reading it's because you want to know as much as possible to start this great adventure "TODAY". From the time I started and shared this book on Amazon to this very day where my life is truly blissful it feels like a magical fairy tale. I am now adding and sharing with you the path not just mine but other amazing light workers that have came across my path. One online friend asked me Daisy what is "THE SECRET" to being a successful psychic. "The secret to your success".

It all started with an intention "Sage Goddess said".

I was a dream that I could not pass up, that awoke me night after night "Daisy said".

It's just what I have always known I was supposed to do. Do any of these voices sound like yours? Today you will start your path. Today you will put your intention. After all you are a spiritual being of life and light. Everything you need is there all you have to do is take action.

Message from the angels:

"You have wonderful ideas don't allow past bumps in the road keep you from your progress, clear up communication problems. We are here for you and eagerly wait for your intention and decisions. Archangel Michael.

Believe in yourself latent within take a moment to hear the voices in your heart that is us. Do what brings you joy, joy is the way of life. Through joy you live a blessed and prosperous life if it doesn't bring you joy then look for a new way. Archangel Metatron.

Life is a reason to celebrate imagine meeting friends for tea and doing great things within your community starting your very own meditation group or angel classes today is the day. Take out the notebook and write everything you hear within. These are the guided steps you need to take. I see happy announcement regarding great success. Don't wait, now is the moment, now is all you need; and "Now" is all you have. Leave yesterday in the past and tomorrow to your angels as you work joyously "Now" today. Archangel Raphael."

These last few months since this very book launched I have witness miracles in my life. Some of my own but I have seen many of you that have crossed paths with me change in such harmonious positive and magical ways. Thank you for your love and support, thank you for sharing my messages and my purpose with the world.
Love
Daisy

Secret Spiritual fairy remedy for manifesting:
Message from the fairies
"Dear ones as the new moon rises you ground yourself get down within the dirt and align your we bodies with the dirt. Take off your shoes knees in ground and hands on grass. It's time to regroup

your inner non-sense and take back what has always been yours. You are a divine being and you are worth everything you dream of. Do you know you dreams are real and you are the only reason they are not manifested. You will sit under the new moon light and you will ask the goddess of the moon your intention. Go ahead speak your mind ask what you want what you seek within your life. Now be specific no doubts please as this is real as you and me. Now mother earth is grounding you with healing properties beyond your years so sit tight as she aligns you with the Universe delights. Within this lovely night bring flower essence to your home as you take pieces of the land on your voyage to this dream come true plan. Light your energy with colors of earthly choice, blues, greens, browns inner guidance is your voice. It is very important that you believe it's all yours and that once your intention is set you release it to us the fairies of the land for our magik is fun and creative and we are but a click ways from your dense climate and boundaries. Within our realm all is well and we see only light and solutions to our plans. Give us yours and watch the wondrous days play joyfully in

Un-expected ways."

Mark your calendar and make the date organize yourself to create this intention of your desires of becoming a successful psychic. What branch are you trying to manifest? What is your purpose on this quest? Be specific and true to you because once you put the intention under the moon all will rise like you have never witnessed before.

Materials:

A candle (seven day is great)
Earth colors, blue, green, brown but you can use reds and oranges as well.

Flowers: again use flowers that call upon you, seek Flower therapy for different flower properties and elements as you want to create a truly manifesting alignment of this most powerful night. Incense, spiritual perfumes and scents like Florida water, Patchouli is great as essential oil soaps because of its attraction elements.

Be creative go to a spiritual shop and see what calls your attention follow your intuition this magical spiritual awakening is a lesson in knowing you hold the key to all your desires. Read the message of the fairies over and over to understand the truth that lies within all of us. We all hold the key to our success. What to do:

On the night of the new moon with all your spiritual remedies write down your intention or intentions. I like to focus on 2 intentions no more no less. There is no right or wrong go with the flow after all you are creating your path.

Be specific no how to just what you want. The angels the fairies God the universe will take care of the how to. YOU just be open to the synchronicity that will follow this night.

Sit in the ground kneeling no shoes you and the ground in perfect alignment is getting down and dirty. Pour your heart out speak your voice. One of the first (many times) I did this I cried because it was such a beautiful and emotional loving experience. You will feel the connection of you and the mother core. When you are finished go inside ad light your candle put your intention note under your lit candle. Leave it for the time the candle burns. On the last day or night of your candle burn the paper and say I release my intention to you Universe I know this is already here "NOW". And so it is.

Burn in a safe place spread the ashes over the land.

Again outside no shoes totally grounded. Now go back in and start the process. Even now after you burn your intention by giving it to the universe you will have started receiving insight and action plans.

There is no wrong or right act upon your inner guidance.

This is the secret you are the answer it's all within you so take action steps. Act upon the guidance the angels are showing you. Remember you hold the key to your life God will send you all you need but you must act first.

Follow my YouTube channel for guidance and upcoming live events where I share new success stories and Manifesting with the fairy messages.

Remember you hold the key to your life God will send you all you need but you must act first.

More, working as an online psychic idea:

As I grow I love to come back to my books and share the many ways I create in a giving format so like yourself; you can create a SUCCESSFUL WAY OF LIFE. (Key #11)

Today I have an ever-growing etsy shop where I now I sell my readings, meditations, full moon release, fertility, un-blockings. Then there are my spiritual spells which consist of oils herbs and candles. My art and spiritual messages, among creative ways the angels inspire me to share.

My etsy shop sells my items and links to my Face book page and my oranum page. This is a great way to circle your work.

You want to take pictures of your work with detail, add pretty spiritual backgrounds.

 Also my expanding Fairy Garden that now belongs to my wonderful Father where I can come back and forth to do many of my weekly readings; for my YouTube channel.

When creating your etsy Shop find a name that stands out and has at least one word for what you are selling. Then be descriptive when adding items, another great idea is adding your goodies in more than one language. This might be more work, yes but the outcome is flowingly. Not only do I sell my goodies in my etsy shop but in my eBay too. Create a name for yourself by providing free shipping for your online friends. Another great idea is everyone loves to receive their readings in the mail. I provide FREE SHIPPING and send them a blissful message adorned with herbs and colored wax, along with spiritual remedies. You can see some of my work in the picture below. Create a beautiful name for yourself online for if you don't work on Oranum today you know that they are eagerly looking for your loving messages on face book. Or ordering your delightful words on etsy and eBay, the idea is that you take action and do that which will bring you "JOY" and success. This adorable bottle goes around your neck to hold a special protection, love remedy, healing, or abundance. I

sell them on etsy and eBay.

You can do this, just take action and start today.

Feel free to message me any questions I love to

engage in conversation. And helping others

become spiritual and work from home is one of my

life purposes.

February 17, 2014 Today "The muse" is no longer it is "Secrets to Work at Home Success: A

complete Guide to starting your own business, balance work and home life, secrets to a successful WAHM
" The thing is I was "The Muse" if you know what the legend of the muse is she gives all the inspiration but doesn't take anything for herself. I asked my angels what am I. Who am I?

http://www.amazon.com/Secrets-Work-Home-Success-successful-ebook/dp/B00DXH6ZUG/ref=sr_1_2?ie=UTF8&qid=1397968848&sr=8-2&keywords=daisy+fabelo

"You are a spiritual teacher born Indigo within this lifetime but a true mystic angel, as you have been here many times. You are to teach others and you must learn to accept the gifts life has in store for you. Reach out and accepts all the gifts God sends you "NOW". It took me a while to soak all this in. I am not who I thought to be. They are right I do not know how to accept the help I truly deserve. It

wasn't until I learned to say "NO" when I didn't want to do something, and "thank you" when I was offered help, and gifts, that I became the truly successful being I am "NOW". I live a blessed life but it did not happen overnight. I had to get to a certain point to know what I had to do. Today I am FREE because I focus on today. I write I do readings, paint, and my artistic spiritual remedies. I enjoy being able to do everything I truly LOVE without any worries about SALES, because I know God and the angels will take care of all behind the scenes. How did I learn this way? Through meditation, reading everything, being open to expanding and living in the "NOW" moment, as my true self. You can read all about abundance and prosperity in my book "7 key steps to living the life you dream".

http://www.amazon.com/Steps-Living-your-Dream-Life-ebook/dp/B00F7GYZ5I/ref=sr_1_3?ie=UTF8&qid=1397968848&sr=8-3&keywords=daisy+fabelo

The secret to a psychic's success=INTENTION

We are always seeking the how to success guide or plan. We don't know we hold that power within ourselves. Each few months this very book grows, expands with new tips, success stories insights, ideas, and links among many other concepts.

Still you are here because you want to know exactly "HOW TO BECOME A SUCCESSFUL PSYCHIC."

RIGHT????

Here is a message The Angels would like to share with you. *"You must want it. You must act upon it. You must seek help and when the help arrives accept it. You must be still. You must know it is already yours and grab the abundance, the prosperity, the joy. You must be HAPPY NOW!!!! You must feel abundant NOW!!!! Now is what you have Now is all you need. What ideas have come to you this very moment? Write them down and act upon them NOW!!! Do not leave NOW for the future, or leak yesterdays failures into this moment. Now you are successful. Now others seek what you have to offer. Live this moment and all will magically arrive NOW because Now is all we have."*

Part two: creative branches of the psychic industry:

Psychic success eBook Start your own psychic classes.(key # 12)

 Starting your own psychic classes is a very genuine way to not only open up into a whole new cliental. That will want you to do readings for them but also to make a nice steady income through teaching others what comes naturally to you. Get creative do these classes in your home, if you have access to a FREE club house, park, anywhere you can teach at a set class price but doesn't charge you to rent the space to start. As your classes grow then you can expand outward into either a spiritual shop where you can split the profits with the owner or really expand by opening your very own.

(key # 13)A great idea is through psychic fairs, local festivals, and events where you can be on a brochure and your business is LOUD and CLEAR. The foot traffic alone will talk the abundance flow. Set of a Fair with a lovely tent be CREATIVE. Add curtains for private readings, take your spiritual remedies, books, oils, incense, oracle cards, spiritual paintings. There are so many different things you can sell and do in a psychic fair but the best outcome is NEW online friends plus people will love to interact with you. Make sure you have plenty of business cards ready to give away if they don't read with you or (IF YOU ARE TOO FULL) there's always tomorrow.

(key #14)Readings as an entertainer you see great group readers like the famous Theresa Caputo. If you Google psychic entertainers you will see an array of different psychics that use their talents through social gatherings and events. One of the websites that I found a psychic was offering her services as follows:

"Do you want to give your event that extra "wow"? Psychic entertainment is sure to be a party pleaser. For small events, required minimum of 6 people, each of your guests will receive a 15 to 20 minute reading for $25.00 per person. If you don't have six people, just plan on the minimum charge of $150.00 for your party. Whichever type of reading you choose for your guests –handwriting, psychic or intuitive readings– these 15-20 minute sessions provide encouragement and inspiration by identifying areas of strength and addressing specific questions.

Simply set aside a private room or quiet place for the readings with two comfortable chairs and a table. Plan a little food and drink, and then invite some friends to your home or office for an intriguing experience! As a psychic entertainer I'll be sure to make your event one to remember."

Imagine working just through the weekend and making $150.00 per party I also saw other psychic entertainers making $125.00 per hour discount is three hours for $250. Sweet "right"?

You can do this too; all you have to do is be out going and comfortable with yourself. If you have a YouTube channel face book page where you are constantly engaging with other beings you can surely connect within a social event setting. How about small parties like tupp o ware remember those you can do the same Offer FREE reading to the Host and a price per friends BE CREATIVE.

Okay you know the world is shifting new spiritual beings are coming out with new energy waves to creating a life of divinity. The new waves are Tapping this is a healing meditation along with some simple tapping on different parts of your body that is suppose to release suppressed energy, like toxins, stress, tension, old adage that needs to be let go of. I am actually joining the Hay House world summit event of Tapping. I will be posting different blogs on this amazing new wave of healing and creating the abundance, health, love life you desire all by some simple yet potent tapping exercises. You have to understand people want to live their dream lives and we are spiritual healers because with our psychic talents we heal others from inspirational messages and advice to meditation, words that create a wave of "AHA MOMENTS" however you choose to express you talent will shift a new movement; and who knows you might create the next spiritual wave.

There are many new spiritual healing methods that I have used on my clients, YouTube channel earth angels and all over my social gatherings and events.
You all know Joe Vitale from "The Secret" a homeless man who used the law of attraction to live a blissful lavish life. Well Joe knows

has an amazing new way to release old resentment, depression, subconscious residue that has clogged your attraction waves.
It is called "Ho'oponopono"
Which means I am sorry
Please forgive me
I love you
Thank you.
Follow the link to see the just how magical this meditation truly is. How Dr.Hew Len healed a psyche ward of the worst criminals, mental patients using this very **powerful and unique meditation.**

http://www.youtube.com/watch?v=ZTViougNWKo

You hold the key the answers will appear in front of your very eyes all you have to do is open them and your arms to receive what is rightfully yours.

These past few months into 2014 I have met some success stories and like minded earth angels like Rebecca Gilland. Who found an amazing way to expand her spirituality and is now expressing her angelic messages. Her face book page is growing and she is starting a YouTube channel very soon.

https://www.facebook.com/pages/Angel-card-reader/1485611538331205

On this quest and knowledge sharing I met great people and this is another great secret. You must share with others. The reason I invite you to join me and to share yourself on my social networks is because my print and you are completely different. We all have our signature. To be the very best psychic you must know when like doctors you should send your online friends for a second opinion; especially within really personal matters like children and health concerns. You be the judge but know that the law of abundance expands in such a manner that there is more than enough for everyone. These past few months Rebecca and I have started online events and she shares her info on my networks as she starts her own psychic business. We are doing fairy readings together and she helps on my weekly live events.

A great way to gather an audience is through LIVE EVENTS. You engage on themes and topics that will cause interaction and flow. By getting together with other psychics you grow together and create larger word of mouth energy. This is a wave you want to create. You will be helping someone with their own work and the Universe will provide you with surplus

venues.

These upcoming months my books go into print and I will be traveling through festivals where I will be doing readings, and speaking engagements. YOU CAN DO THIS TOO.

Simply Google festival craft shows in your area this alone will bring you online friends and promote you time after time as the news will spread, especially if you repeat certain venues. I go to a local monthly festival where people know me by name and come for readings, spells, herbs, spiritual remedies and my new venture spiritual healing art work.

 I create art with herbs and essential oils along with different paints. I add inspirational messages sometimes personal pictures. Creating vision board art for online friends or fertility healing art, the ideas are endless and make me happy to work upon my purpose with passion. Ask yourself, what is your passion?

You know I love to write though my grammar sucks my books inform and inspire others to follow their dreams. This is exactly why they come to my videos to begin with inspiration what am I doing different. The truth is you will have to find your own way but use my experience to experience yours.

Does that make sense? When I share success stories is because these psychics have inspired me and I learn from their work. One of the messages I received from my angels was seek like minded individuals that will teach you. This is what you will do explore your world by finding others doing what you would like to do. You won't copy them because like I explained before we all have our signature. You will grow by being your authentic self. Your authentic self is the passionate person that is not just here because you want to make lots of money but because you want to do something that makes you untimely happy.

Example sometimes the spiritual remedies I have for my online friends are not sold. Therefore I created an etsy shop where I can sell exactly what I recommend and if I don't have it then I send them to other online friends that do.

This is one of the fairy gardens created by my dad where I grow herbs

for my spells and events. I also share lots of pictures you want to be personal with your online friends. To see where you work, what you do make them feel comfortable with you.

My videos are loved when they are in my garden or next to the beach that I adore. This creates a beautifully energetic atmosphere for my spiritual readings and work. Especially that I do a lot of one on one personal work. When I give a reading it is done with the upmost energy. If you already "LIVE" the psychic life you know this job can drain your energy therefore it is very important that your area is always at the highest of frequencies. This is why I love working outdoors. Who better to protect and enfold me than the angels and fairies?

Another awesome success story:

Lisa Beachy I first met Lisa looking for meditations back in 2011. Her meditations are my favorite she resonates with my energy in ways that engulf my spirituality. Lisa Beachy has meditations for every circumstance and issues and adding and growing.

https://www.youtube.com/user/MeditationsforMoms

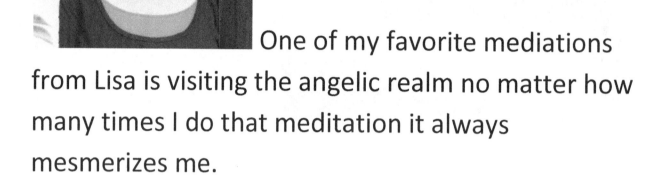One of my favorite mediations from Lisa is visiting the angelic realm no matter how many times I do that meditation it always mesmerizes me.

You see as a successful psychic you need to grow spiritually you need to always be learning especially that in many ways you are a teacher. It is a give and take an exchange of energies. If you do this you will be a successful psychic follow your intuition let this little messy eBook simple guide the light that is already there.

Grow your herbal gardens within or outside your homes. Light up your altars be creative in all ways.

Teach what you learn and share your growth because everyone deserves to be as successful as you will be from this moment on.

"*The secret*" *key # 15*

I noticed over the many years of creating this easy abundant life setting was by letting go. Being me and not fighting. What this means and it will take lots of practice, is you must allow. Example I use to dress in black because Black was the color of thin. Today I am happily beautiful in my over 150 lbs. I wear the spiritual colors my guide's advice due to the changing of the world. I listen to my guides THAT ARE THE SECRET be open and aware to the signs.

In the law of attraction it say ASK THE UNIVERSE be SPECIFIC and ALLOW. Let me break that down. ASK for what you want describe in detail. "I want to be a successful online psychic." Okay so you asked Now say. "Please send me CLEAR SIGNS". You want the

Universe to work for you that is the Universal Law. God has a plan a purpose, you have a driven life but sometimes we are so BUSY trying that we don't see. If we simply step back and just ALLOW things to come our lives would be easier.

Now let's put it into elementary words. I asked the Universe for a successful life as a psychic because I love my work. Now in 1999 if you would have told me I was going to be living my dream life while helping others with theirs I would have laughed at you. Why because I didn't see how easy abundance just flows. I do not worry about paying bills and I have not for a long time, because I know God pays my bills.

When we try to hard Like ex. (I won't say any names) there's a psychic on my face book page who pushes for others to do readings with her, she's certified as an angel therapist. Yet she doesn't have the online friends she wishes she had. WHY?

Because she is pushing this is how I do it.

I post my new items, reading prices, and then I go do other things like my YouTube channel, writing my books, among the many things I do daily. My PayPal rings you have a reading I go do that reading. My YouTube channel rings you have a reading, I go do that one. POINT= if you are just sitting waiting for someone to do readings for you. Your stopping the FLOW allows the readings to come to you by engaging in other things.

Here's the hardest one. When I first stated receiving money from readings was so TABOO. WOW you have a gift from God and you are charging. You're definitely going to hell. This is exactly what I was told. Doctors are healers yet the get paid pretty nice for healing. Why are you and I so different? We are not so move on. I have met many whose EGO doesn't allow them to RECEIVE or they feel they OWE everyone. Now we can all open FREE READING face book pages and I guarantee you will be out of energy and not capable to doing anything else. Your page will have 1000's among the many who need your guidance but what about you? What are you getting = attention. Well if that puts food on your table then blessings to you.

In the beginning I was just like that. Friends would call me in the mid hours of the night because their husbands left. "Oh Daisy what do the angels say will he come home tonight"? I would stay with them ask the angels and guide. The thing was after a few months of bed rest because I was spiritually dehydrated. The angels said Daisy No more readings. They were firm I was giving my all.

To Do: Today I give FREE MINI readings unless it's a dire need and the angels seek my help. This is a great way to show your talent and to GIVE. I know the universe will send me my gifts I eagerly await the beautiful arrays they arrive in.

Mini readings are a great way to get someone to seek your future guidance and others to say "Wow I love the way Daisy's messages speak" = new online friends. You can be nice to those that don't have enough or cut some discounts to your regulars. I do I love my online best-ies but I still receive.

YOU TOO!!!! Don't feel guilt because that is a negative energy and stops the flow of abundance.

And never call your online friends CLIENTS you are smashing the personal connection. I see my online friends as earth angels who eagerly await their own guidance to fulfilling their purpose. I guide them so they can fulfill. I am fulfilled and the universe circles. Thank you for reading, sharing and enjoying my work. I wish you the very best on your endeavors and I know you will live up to your dream destiny of a successful psychic.

The best advice I can possibly give, the best secret to my success and the one I am always working upon is being true to me. That is your success to be you and only you from this moment on.

If you are seeking daily inspiration and angelic message visit "ANGELIC SPIRIT" when I first met Lizabeth she was eagerly sharing angel messages and inspiring me and everyone else in between. Today Angelic has thousands of members in her group and she has to turn some away due to the massive amount of visits and readings. I see a book contract for Angelic and I personally go to her for my readings as I recommend her to all my face book

friends. She is truly an amazing earth angel.
https://www.facebook.com/AngelicSpirit11

 Her work is just lovely she works with crystals and stones. The messages that Flow through this truly inspiring angel are WOW.

What will your success story be? Where do you see yourself next year today?

Make the goals be ambitious about your dreams you deserve everything and more. Now what are you waiting for "START".

Oh and be nice leave me a nice review because I deserve it TOO."

Love

Daisy Fabelo

Mystic angel. *About the author:*

Daisy Fabelo is an online spiritual advisor, writer, psychic entertainer, mom of three awesome kids, and three beautiful grand-daughters; wife to an amazing husband, and author of three successful best-selling books.

She has made her successful living by being a mystic angel messenger to others. Her life is serving the children on GOD, "you". Her purpose is guiding, inspiring you to find your personal dream life by doing what you love and loving what you do every single day. When Daisy's not writing painting working online she is enjoying her beach home with her loving family that she feels is the greatest gift of her life. You can find Daisy through her various channels but she's mostly on her face book "Mystic Angel Readings and Spiritual advice".

Made in the USA
Las Vegas, NV
02 December 2023

81962690R00044